Carmichael Speaks

Carmichael Speaks

Spiritual Expression, Life Experience, Memoriam

William Fletcher Carmichael

Copyright © 2021 by William Fletcher Carmichael.

Library of Congress Control Number:	2021914980
ISBN: Hardcover	978-1-6641-8673-6
Softcover	978-1-6641-8672-9
eBook	978-1-6641-8671-2

All rights reserved. No part of this book may be reproduced or transmitted in any form or by any means, electronic or mechanical, including photocopying, recording, or by any information storage and retrieval system, without permission in writing from the copyright owner.

Any people depicted in stock imagery provided by Getty Images are models, and such images are being used for illustrative purposes only.
Certain stock imagery © Getty Images.

Print information available on the last page.

Rev. date: 07/22/2021

To order additional copies of this book, contact:
Xlibris
844-714-8691
www.Xlibris.com
Orders@Xlibris.com
810196

Contents

Leaving	1
Music	2
I Need Not Know	3
Mankind Oneness	5
Jeremiah Thoughts	6
Moses Wife	7
Whereforth Am I	9
God's Gift	12
O Gates Of Hell	13
Wasted Time	17
Enmity	21
The Unbiased Christ	23
The Story of Easter	25
Praise Through Poetry	27
Forgive Us	29
No Drugs/Jesus	33
Just What I Needed	35
The Pearl of a Girl	36
Gabriel Blow Your Trumpet	37
Reborn	40
Christmas Thoughts	41
Is Religion Right?	43
Rejoice My Beloved	44
We Shall Build God's House	47
Reign With Him	48
Christian Love slave	49
Doorkeeper	50
Missionary	52

History in Poetry

Memories Of Our Barn	59
Frolly Gee	60

Chill Man Chill	61
Columbus	63
What is Black	64
Deception	66
Thank You Toussaint	67
Freedom	68
Pro-Lynched	69
Who Am I?	70
Moving Ahead	73
Contributus	74
Colors	76
I Tell You A Truth	77
Proud to be Black	80
Value of a Man	82
Blackman, Negro, or Colored Boy	83
Glutton's Revival	85
Jim Beckwourth	86
Don't You Know Me	87
Bill Pickett	89
Escape	90
Episode of the Mind	92
Parenthood	94
Vision	95
A Man	96
Dr. Charles Drew	97
My Family	98
Good Father, My Father	100
Share Cropper Prayer WFC	102
Abolitionist	103
Barack Obama	104
From Hawaii	105
My Grandson	106
Just A Man	107
In Time	109
Hall To The Chief	110

White House Days 111
Most Moral President 112
Barry/Barack 113
In My Dreams 114

I Remember You

Appreciation 119
A Gift 120
Just A Mortal Man 122
Excellency 124
Aurevoir Aurevoir 126
Sister Martha Smallwood 127
A Concerned Daughter 128
Sarah Margaret 130
Reflections To Aunt Francis McLean 132
Memories Of Bro. Stewart 134
James (Jim) Bowens 135
Deacon Henry Brown 137
Harvey McCallum 138
A Crown of Glory 139
A Sermon 140
Just A Mortal Man 142
Miss Polly 144
The Journey's End 145
To My Darling Grandmother 146
Mother 148
Dorothy (Ford) Lee 149
Burden Carrier 150
Until 151

About the Author 153

Fletcher, Sam and Houston

Leaving

12-28-19

God did not take me away from you
He received me unto hisself
The one who took me away from you
His name is known as death

The sorrow you feel at this time
Is not by you alone
I too am sorrowful to leave
But full of joy I'm going home

The angels are awaiting me
To do what I've done best
In heaven it will not be a job
Entering into my rest
I love you all
Be Blessed!!!

Music

10-13-2020

God gave a gift to Tubal Cain
To make a musical sound
Thousands of years later
Someone wrote a sound down

Today we call it music
It spreads the whole world round
From Beethovan to Michael Jackson
Great men have worn it's crown

It is a language of the heart
A blind man can compose
From poverty to riches
Gifted ones have arose

It has created industries
In every language and tongue
From song to intruments
Poems and prose have been sung

Love is the key that music turns
To open angry hearts
Music will calm the savage beast
At least it makes a start.

I Need Not Know

(1968)

I need not know much physics
And just a portion of math
To walk this rugged journey
Along this rocky path

I do know Christ Jesus
I know of Him quite well
I know that He shall one day
Save my soul from hell

For me it shall be glorious
My heart shall overflow
For I shall be with Jesus
Forever and ever more

If I had been given the problem
of man's salvation
I could not have carried it through
For you and I were divided in sin
And death is the dividend due
But Christ the great mathmetician
Solved it and carried it through
Transposing eternal life
To those who are born anew

Jesus the great physicist
turned water into wine
caused the lame to walk
Even gave sight to the blind

Jesus the great politician
Was not elected by men
By God the Father He was chosen
To pay the price for sin

That's why I need not know man's way
If I trust in Jesus Christ
Knowing there is no other way
To receive eternal life.

Mankind Oneness

From one blood come all mankind
All of yours all of mine
With the first man and woman
Creation did shine
Our Creator has never ever been blind
Rich and poor black and white
Bloodlines in us are all alike
Regardless of color of skin
Humanity from two did begin
One earthly race of men.

Jeremiah Thoughts

11/1/13   by WFC   Jer. Chapter 38:7

Ebed Meleck said brother, "Where you at"
"I'm down here in this hole in the ground
Been days since you've come around
So quiet down here I can't hear a sound
Except the thump thump of the ground."

"Speak to the prince, speak to the queen
Speak to the king about this thing
My cough sounds like I'm about to die
I need to be fed; I need to get dry
I need sunshine from the open sky

The king don't know just what they've done
I'm a Jew, I'm a prophet, I'm one of God's sons
My punishment is so extreme
Make your way and tell the king
He doesn't know, he doesn't know

This pit, this hole gets mighty cold
I'm dripping wet from head to toe
Ethiopian, Ethiopian tell the king these evil mens' plan
A prophet's death will be on your hands
Deliver me, to life again.

Moses Wife

In response to John Bunyan's (16-28-88)"
of Moses Wife

Moses had a black wife
Yes he did
To their union God blessed them
They birth two kids
Two young Jewish - black, men
To help us all, fight sin
Moses had a black wife
Yes he did

Sin is not black
It's crimson red
Moses swarthy black wife
Could soothe his weary head
Sin is not black
It's crimson red

God approved of Moses wife
To her family he was led
God approved of Moses wife
Becoming one they both shared one bed
God approved of Moses wife
She saved his mortal life

She circumcised her baby son
She respected his holy life
God approved of Moses black wife

God blessed the Ethiopian
The wisdom her father did bring

God blessed the Ethiopian
God blessed her offsprings
Moses was thought Egyptian king
God gave him a princess of Midian
Moses married a black wife
A beautiful woman of black
Healthy skin
Yes he did, yes he did

Whereforth Am I

(1970)

O' rature reaching to yonder skies
O' solice of the silent cries
O' place that dwelleth, deep my soul
Whereforth am I where now my goal

O' measures of mediocrity
O' salvation, reality
O' Jesus spirit close to me
Whereforth am I give sight to see

O' Plights of life within a man
O' Wisdom, I cannot understand
O' Fears I know and fears unknown
Whereforth am I, sing now, my song.

Omni-present God that sees and knows
Show me now the way to go
Mark the path of righteousness
Now here I be but like a mist
A cloud that the wind doth drive away
As grass that withereth by heat of day
A vapor that seemeth to dissappear
Give ear my soul, give ear to hear

Hear now my soul and do rejoice
Let not my spirit sense remorse
There now exist calamity
But above the skies there's victory

O' Watchful eye that ever stares
O' Rapture rapture, rapture somewhere
Come down to earth, come close to me
That these mine eyes, that they may see

Somewhere my soul that I speak of
Somewhere my heart so filled with love
My thoughts they cannot comprehend
This soul of love that dwells within

O' Equal forces of universe
Must I to man, must I rehearse
Somewhere I'm real, somewhere I'm true
Whereforth am I, this residue
O' lively stones of Jesus Christ
O' Ministers of eternal life
Come now forth, from depths of soul
Come now forth, proclaim your goal
Possess your soul by spirit control
In this your life conduct your role
Be not tossed to and fro
But stedfast evermore

A bit of emotions convinces the flesh
But it cannot assure you happiness
The peace of the spirit and it alone
Can in your heart compose a song

The joy of living isn't happiness
But tis journeying on to reach your quest
To know that you've achieved your goal
No matter how grievous to the soul
The life that Christ requires of us

Has an eternal purpose
Embodied in Christ's spiritual life
Whereforth am I, I am in Christ

Be still my soul and hear God speak
Be strong my soul, O' be not weak
I'll be renewed within my mind
I'll never faint nor fall behind
The race is not given to the swift
Our victory tis all a gift
The master predestinated our roles
He paid the price to save our souls

Whereforth am I?
This hour, this day.
I am not lost, I'm on my way
I'm reaching the Father who is above
Through faith in Christ which works by love

God's Gift

05-23-2007

YOU ARE NOT ANOTHER ME
AS I THOUGHT YOU WOULD BE
GOD SENT YOU TO ADD TO ME
THE PARTS NEEDED TO MAKE COMPLETE
THE MISSING MEMBERS DESIGNED FOR ME

GOD MAKES US PARTS OF HIS PLAN
I NEED YOU TO HELP ME STAND
YOU NEED ME TO HELP YOU SEE
WE BOTH ARE PARTS OF ETERNITY
EACH HELPING EACH TO BE

GOD SENT ME TO YOU AND YOU TO ME
I AM NOT "ALL THAT" AS I CLAIM TO BE
GOD GAVE YOU GOD GAVE ME
GOD GAVE BEFORE UPON A TREE
HIS BLOOD OF LIFE WHICH WE NOW BLEED
WE ARE PARTS OF CREATIVITY
TO FORM ANOTHER MAN LIKE HE
MEMBERS OF THE BODY TO BE
I HELPING YOU YOU HELPING ME
FORMING SINGULARITY
ONE GOD IN PARTS OF THREE
IS HE

O Gates Of Hell

(1967)

Draw near me not O gates of hell
O' Flattery woman, O' devil's snare
O' Foul and evil tounge of death
Try not to obstruct my well mastered path

O' Evil corruption O' grim and dirt
Why leadeth thy body by sin besmirched
Cast lust and temptation aside, cast it away
God forbid this body to let it stay

O' depraved, tainted, and putrid man
Who created and founded this desolate land
Now, like an ant crawleth ye upon the ground
Where is thy God, his pleasant sound

Call forth the fowl that flieth by day
The lamb of the flock which has gone astray
Green pastures, green pastures, somewhere there must be
Open my eyes, my God, let me see

Open my eyes, I must know to survive
Great are the supplications of endurance I strive
O mighty, merciful, loving God
Make strong and useful my staff and rod

O death I cry, O God just why
I know I've sinned, why must I die
Immortal matter, earth and space abound
I, I man, must return to the ground

Lifted up above all things else
To be dropped, dropped so lowly down
Unless, unless I have an immortal soul
What is my purpose, what is my goal,
Unless I have an imortal soul

My God, my God, before thee I cry
For surely someday to the earth I must die
But yet, O yet while larynx car utter a tone
I shall cry to the heavens, to thee all day long

O blow ye winds from shore to shore
Cleanse me from sin now and ever more
O' body of clay, sin drenched within
By the blood of Jesus let me be cleansed

Yes God is around me and yet I cry
For fearing death, I fear to die
Those gates of hell they open so wide
While, I so weak, being forced inside

The Lord is my shepherd, my master and guide
He knoweth the self I try to hide
Why permitteth thine agony, thine agony and pain
My heart has suffered but love not slain

The sluggard goeth to the ant, considereth it's ways and are wise
Whereforth God hath I to turn, when ignorance doth abide
A child of God, in the eyes of man is a fool in everyway
Our thoughts hopes and future are not of this land of clay

The theif goeth to the jeweler, takes pride in his swiftness of hands
The child of God, upon this earth, for what materialistic thing do we stand

While heaven .... yet so far away
We must have faith have faith and pray

Our treasures are where our hearts doth dwell
Mine, things of this earth which draineth near hell
Not that they aren't good to use
But they are truly the devils tools

Is that why, the kingdom of heaven is where our hearts should be
Instead of worldly things which troubleth me?
Therefore God you must surely care
If you'll open your kingdom that I might share.

O' God I've heard thy holy word spoken
I, a sinner, fell down on my knees and wept
Mine heart was totally broken
Yet I've been hung by the devil's snare
Release me O' God, if thou dost care.

Fortitude, peace, O' victory
Come closer to shore, come closer to me
Failure I am and failure I've been
I'm headed for hell for I'm in sin

O' God if thou dost hear a sinners prayer
Hear this, of repentence from the devil's snare
O' hell I fear you, O' heaven I hear you
Somehow I know there's no in between
Yet, I am man, and man sometimes doubt
Sometimes doubt what the eye hasn't seen

Let me know, dear God, what you would have me do
Mine heart is sincere mine heart is true
Let me know dear God what you would have me do

Like driftwood upon the sea destined nowhere
This life of mine has been, led directly by the devil's snare

Draw near me not O' gates of hell
For there's a better place, where souls shall dwell
I now, want to change and be in that number so great
Fed by the great shepherd, of God's word they ate
Save, some are still eating, even until this day
While others ignorant as I have drifted astray
Draw near me not, O' gates of hell!!

Wasted Time

(1970)

A young boy went out
to play one day
He saw an old man,
Across the way
Sitting alone,
With hair all grey
The young boy looked
At his toys in play
And said, "I wonder if these
would brighten his day."
Looked again at
The man's hair so grey
Then slowly turned
As to walk away

A thought came in
The young boy's mind
Yet he thought it foolish
To waste the man's time
But as a boy
He obeyed his mind

Now standing still
Near the old man's face
The young boy seemed
So out of place
He sought for words
Some words to say
Still all words seemed
To fade away

He thought of when
He was over there playing
This is what
He ended up saying:
"Sir,
Tell me what
Makes a man grow old?
Where on me
Is my soul?"

The man looked up
So stunned to see
A young boy asking
Such questions as these

The wrinkled face,
Began to smile
His mind extended
For miles and miles

"Mommy says, I will grow old,
Mommy says, I have a soul"

The man sought deeply
Within his mind
Yet answers to these
He could not find

The smile then
Turned into a frown
The old man reached
Toward the ground
The old man's eyes
Seemed to grow cold

His voice was quivering
His speech was slow:

"Son, I've lived many days
Now I am old
I didn't know
I had a soul
Until a little while ago
I'm sorry son
I just don't know

When I was young
About your age
All I ever did was played
Son,
I've wasted so many days
All I know
To do is pray
That God will wipe
My sins away

When you grow up
To be a man
Keep asking questions
To understand
That you might help
Reveal God's plan

To help some child
Become a man
So when your hair
Is grey as mine
You won't feel that
You've wasted time

You'll have an answer
For little boys
When they grow weary
Of playing toys
You'll have the wisdom
With the years
Instead of memories and tears.

Enmity

(1967)

The eyes of enmity beholdeth my soul
The forces of evil host wrought control
The good intentions intended to do
Could change this enmity
Be twixt me and you
Now doth enmity behold my soul
And evil devices my hands do mold.

I caught a glimpse of a glidding dove
then enmity seemed to cast out love
An innocent stone laying near at hand
Destroy, destroy was devil's command
the glidding dove it's wings did fold
O' why must enmity behold my soul

Collapsing forces O' powers unknown
Chant not to me the devils songs
Fill not my heart with hatred and fear
Till the voice of enmity is all I hear
lead not my soul to destruction and wrong
Till my dwelling place is the devils home

Bewitching powers now beguile my soul
The forces of enmity hast taken control
I fear not what I think to do
Mine thoughts are harmless through and through
the forces of evil, of filth of dirt,
Hast governed my deeds to my own hurt

I polluted the air which filled the sky
To be God of the world to rule on high
Enmity shaped a mind of thoughts
Destruction, destruction, is what it wrought
Pollution of air of mind, of soul
till wrath hast stolen my heavenly goal

Is that a scripture, a scripture before me
A way of truth, of light, of peace
O' gather these thoughts that I behold
that I might feast and save my soul
Toss all understanding within my heart
So light can seep into the dark

The God of love is close to me
Thus away with this enmity
Let peace and joy control my soul
Let peace and joy become my code
The powers of love are precious and dear
Much greater than this enmity
I used to fear

In the beginning was the love of God
Then enmity fell from beyond the stars
A host of angels and the devil himself
Schemed ways to hide the righteous path
Yet truth and righteousness though buried so deep
Posessed a greater power than enmity

The Unbiased Christ

From a Jew, not a Greek
Though people were mixed in that time
Jesus, a descendant of King David,
Was born of a royal line.

Greek blood wasn't bad,
Plato was their kin.
Jesus, was of a Jew
He was born to bring a newness in

A seed sent down the span of time
A promise long said to be
A hope who would inspire mankind
Throughout eternity.

He came to bring racial harmony
Yet He, non-racial, one blood
Accomplished this in Christianity
A new race of people born in love.

A new love on the face of earth
Agape; it is called
A love of God which puts down none
Breaking down all racial walls

If you can forget color of skin
Of whatever differences may be
Seeing Jesus as our only Father
Then true blood brothers are we

His Father was not a Jew
God almighty as you know
Who lives forever by spirit, not blood
By the spirit we all should grow
From the love of Jesus Christ,
In each born again soul below,
In even those who believe not
No matter our difference, our goal, our plot.

The Story of Easter

(1967)

This is another Easter Sunday my friends
And Christ Jesus truely has risen again
As He does each and every day.
He has lifted us up a step higher
In the righteous way.

I stand before you as new as spring
My heart inside is bursting to sing
It gives me joy to see today
That your heart too,
Feels the very same way.

So we care not for the clothes we wear
Wherther our shoes are new or last years pair
We're just so happy to be here today
Until we put not clothes
But our hearts on display

So let us rejoice and let us give praise
For Jesus Christ had been dead for days
But He conquered death without a spot of sin
To return to heaven where the Father reigns

While here on earth He was misunderstood
Some didn't believe and He knew they never would
Yet there were many whose eyes were blind
He had to heal them or they would be left behind

So He spoke God's word which had the power
So that what was his would also be ours

He was their light, He was their way
And He's every bit the same today

Some thought He came to show His miracles to us
His coming had a much much greater purpose
King of the Jews they said He would be
Yet they crucified Him on Calvary

So what will it be my friends for you
Will you have the mind of an ancient Jew
Crucify Him again on the cross
And care not if your soul be lost?

Don't misunderstand as those of old
For them the story had not completely been told
But for us that are alive and can kneel down and pray
Let us live for Christ each and everyday

Praise Through Poetry

(1973)

Praise through poetry
To me is just a way
To tell the lovers of praise and poems
Jesus lives today

Amidst the crime rates rising
Air and water pollutions
Thousands being killed in wars
Governments with no solutions

Darkness surrounding the earth
Pollution defiling our space
Certainly praise through poetry
Could never be out of place
These precious natural beauties
Escape our eyes, seeming to
While we seek for Godly beauties
From far beyond the skies

We praised through loving nature
The beauty which it displayed
We praised through new inventions
Through creating skits and plays

So why not praise through poetry
Through lyric, verse, and praise
Poetry which seems to inspire the heart
Is so needed in these days

It's true there is no substitute
For the scriptures, are our living bread
But whenever we praise through poetry
That poetry isn't dead

So while we praise through instruments
Through choirs which sing our songs
Let us praise through poetry
For praising is never wrong

Let us praise
To brighten the days
Through scriptures
Poems and songs
Showing beauty through praise
Is where poetry really belongs

WFC

For plays and skits - Matt. 18:15-17
Young men in prison forgive!!

Forgive Us

2000

"Jesus said to forgive the ones who treated you wrong Matt. 5:23"
We do believe what
Jesus said
Forgive the guilty
Don't wish Him dead

Forgive us if we haved sinned
Our race from the African man
You admired us so much
You could not leave us in our land

Forgive us if we have sinned
You came to us in desparation
We treated you like a friend
We were not partial we took you in

Forgive us
Seems like we have offended you
We tried our best not to protest
Through all you put us through

We taught your fathers to comprehend
Our math, our culture, our medicine
Our science which reached unto the stars
We held nothing back, forgive our flaws

Forgive us for understanding Algebra II
When counting was unbeknown too you
Forgive us for houses three stories high
When caves kept you warm and dry

Forgive us if Socrates was fatigued
We taught medicine he did not perceive
T'was never our purpose to offend
Forgive us, if we have sinned

Forgive us for the beauty we do possess
Cleopatra was well blessed
Forgive us for military strategy
Hannibal of Carthage
Holds the key

Forgive us if our ladies didn't fall at your feet
Because of your Caucasoid beauty
We were satisfied with what we had
Forgive us if our minds were iron-clad

Talk to Jehovah, He made Adam and Eve
From Ethiopia they did proceed
He sent Zipporah to Moses side
The Queen of Sheba to be Solomon's guide

Talk to Jesus the king of civility
He can talk to Simon of Cyrene
Read the gospel and understand
Philip and the Ethiopian

Talk to us
Have we contributed to make you great?
Forced to serve, did we serve or fake?
Tell the truth for heaven sake

Talk to your young, then tell them who
Talk of division created by you
Talk of degradation your forefather's plan
When you pretended we were not human
Still faith in God helped us to stand
To show the world we were human

Forgive us if we've offended youth
Our search is only for justice
Our search is only for truth
Our endeavor is to reveal the lies
Hypocrisy in sheep clothing
Concussions delivered by you
Have been generational moulding

Forgive us for having been your slaves
Supplying you with the life you craved
Treating us worse than your dogs
Like animals being kept in a stall
To be released when work wasn't needed
Unless mortality first succeeded

Forgive us for not dying in large numbers
When syphillis was injected our veins didn't crumble
Forgive us for being your experimentations
To solve the problems of your vexations
Forgive us for letting you hang us
For simple misdemeanors
Forgive us for your lying complainers
Unjustly we bare your blame
Unjustly we suffer your shame
Forgive us for being family minded
You bred us like horses for your economy

Seperated husbands, wives and children
Leaving us only with memory
Denying us the rights of nature to family defense
I wonder if God is for or against

Forgive us for loving you in spite of you
With supple breast we nursed
Your daughters and your sons
Forgive us for supporting you
We could have, and did not run
Forgive us for loving you
We died to defend you
On foreign fields our lives did yield
Patriotic and true
Klu-Klux-Klan on home land
Destroying our heroic few

Forgive us for loving you
Time after time forgiving you
Our young men, you kill within
Denying them hope to ascend
Twelve percent our national rate
More deaths, more poor, more prison mates

Forgive us if we have sinned
Forgive us for loving you
For loving our enemy
We believe in Christ's decree
"Love unto all men"

You misjudged Christ, you
Misjudged me
Still you misjudge humanity
We see you do not comprehend
You, you, have sinned
Forgive us if we have offended you.

No Drugs/Jesus

(10-1989)

I need Jesus Christ!!
I don't need no drugs,
To make you think I'm cool,
I need to do my work at home
I need to stay in school
I need to get my education
What it takes to get by,
In the world of the brothers
Green power is the high

I don't need
No marijuana smoke
It can't make me cope
If strung out on dope
I need to take a trade
To marry the foxy babe
To link my family ties
With something greater than the guys
I need Jesus Christ!!

I don't need no drugs
No upper and downer slugs
To give me the gee bee bugs
And turn me into a thieving thug

I need a corporate rug
I need a money plug
I need the spiritual high
What I find in Jesus Christ
I need the love of my fellowman

Not a casual one night stand
I need hope for the sweet by and by
A mansion up there in the sky
I need to know of eternal life
Not just the struggle of cursing strife
I don't need, no drugs!!

I don't need, no drugs
To weaken down my seed
To cripple my unborn
To make me cash on speed
To give me aids through the needle use
To close my veins till they don't produce
To swell my heart like a big balloon
Until it burst and I've died too soon

I don't need no drugs!!
I need Jesus Christ!!
Who gives eternal life

Just What I Needed

(5-23-07)

God makes us part of His plan
I need you to help me stand
You need me to help you see
We both are parts of eternity
Each other helping each other to be

You are not another me
As I thought you would be
God sent you to add to me
The lacking parts which makes complete
The missing members in me

God sent me to you and you to me
I am not "all that" as I claim to be
God gave you, God gave me
God gave before, upon a tree
His blood of life which we now bleed
We are just parts of creativity
To form another man like He
Members of the body to be
I helping you, you helping me
Forming singularity
One God in parts of three, is He.

The Pearl of a Girl

The pearl of a girl is beauty and pride
Those wonderful treasures she holds inside
Eager and anxious to release someday
When from a single fades away

The pearl is more precious than silver or gold
It cannot be bought it cannot be sold
It has an everlasting wealth
Constantly girded by character's belt

Seen, admired, and loved by all
This pearl will never let the girl fall
It will give her elegance
It will give her grace
It shall never let her get out of place

Remember your pearl is precious too
Portray it in all you say or do
So you can be a miracle of a masterpiece
Have pearls galore with joy and peace.

Gabriel Blow Your Trumpet

Eyes have not seen
    Ears have not heard
The multidude of terrible things
    Coming upon the earth

Men hearts shall fail them
    When the evil things come
On that great and terrible day
    They'll try to hide and run

Gabriel blow your trumpet
    Blow it loud and clear
Gabriel blow your trumpet
    Let it be heard by the spiritual ear

All shall perish on that day
    The spiritual shall be saved
God, our Father shall translate
    Us from this body of clay

Gabriel blow your trumpet
    Blow it loud and clear
Gabriel blow your trumpet
    Let believers over the world hear

Blessed are the pure in heart
    Surely they shall be saved
Woe unto the defiled heart
    There is no hiding place

Unimaginable glory
    Christians shall be escorted to
All that is written in the word
    Our Father shall surely do

We have heard the prophets
    There is no doubt in mind
It shall not be very long
    Before the end of time

Gabriel blow your trumpet
    Blow it loud and clear
Gabriel blow your trumpet
    Let even the dead then hear

No time to prepare
    Christ is coming quickly
At the twinkling of an eye's stare
    He shall separate the wicked

Hallelujah, Hallelujah
    We shall sing Hallelujah
Hallelujah, Hallelujah
    We shall sing Hallelujah

Let us shout it to the Father
    Let us shout it to the Son
Let us shout it to the Holy Ghost
    For we and they are one

Gabriel blow your trumpet
    Blow it loud and clear
Gabriel blow your trumpet
    God shall give us the spiritual ear

Heaven won't be far away
    We shall eat from the Tree Of life
Forever we shall go to stay
    We shall live and rule with Christ
We shall have eternal life
    Gabriel blow your trumpet
Gabriel blow your trumpet!!

Reborn

O' blow ye winds of the Holy Ghost
    Through thirsty lands that have no dew,
Through empty valleys and lonely hills,
    In midst of anger-wars, and strife,
The groom hath chosen himself a wife.

O' suctorial pits of satanic hell,
    In midst of thee the devil dwells.
Beneath the earth, above the clouds
    Within the air He placed His wiles
Ashamed to show his truthful face,
    The face of Cain which wears disgrace
An empty valley His soul shall be
    Tormented in pits of eternity.

From midst of a desolate valley, thou came,
    Where the dew had never fallen.
The Holy Ghost blew the dust away,
    Forever a fruitful valley to stay,
Where winds doth blow and dew doth fall
    Where life shall never cease.
Where rivers of water shall find their stalls,
    Forever flowing with joy and peace.
The dust of death by winds shall flee.

Christmas Thoughts

I bid in thoughts of Christmas
With presents beneath the tree
Remember Immanuel
Born for you and me

Betwixt a donkey and a cow
God's only Son was born
Wrapped in swaddling cloth
Born Jesus Christ that day

While angels hovering from heaven above
Within the shepherd's sight
They sung of hallelujah
A child was born that night

The wisemen far away
Were guided by a star
That shone upon a stable
In the land of Judea
With turkey on your tables
With holly on your door
Think of the Christmas origin
A long long time ago

Born unto us a saviour
Not of man's will nor flesh
But of the will of almighty God
He sent unto us his love

Joy Peace on earth good will toward men
The angel did proclaim

A babe wrapped in swaddling clothes
Jesus shall be his name

They came from many distant miles
Bringing gifts to the Holy child
While the news did spread
Through out all Judea
And even through out the Nile

The virgin mother Mary
At last could sigh relief
Her heart now oh so happy
Her flesh no more in grief

With turkey on your tables
And holly on your door
Recall the birth of CHRIST
A long long time ago

RY ???

Is Religion Right?

Is Religion Wrong?
Does it hurt the lonely people?
Does it help the broken home?
Intents of religion are good
As good as can be
Yet even better than religion
Is Christianity

Religions is seeking to find God,
Christianity is God seeking to find Man.
Which has a better chance of success
So tell me now, which is best?

Our creator God, came to us
From his Heavenly home
Lived in this evil world
A world of right and wrong
And finally died for us
To redeem us all from Sin
Completed His work on the third day
When He rose again.

The Christian God is living today
Jesus Christ is his name
He is God incarnate
Not just one who obtained fame
Christianity is a living reality
Religion is just a game.

Rejoice My Beloved

Rejoice my beloved;
I stood afar and I saw thee,
Within my heart I chose thee,
When thou was lost and knew me not,
I gave thee wisdom that thou might fear me.

Rejoice my beloved;
I have seen thy ways of life,
My heart shall make known to thee, I love thee,
Mine eyes have watched thee a long time.
I've come to lift your burdens in life,

Rejoice my beloved;
Yea, I have come to deliver thee,
Suffer ye no more afflictions alone,
Secure thine trust in me, a worthy provider.
While looking from afar I dedicated myself to thee.

Rejoice my beloved;
I ask now your hand
Let our purpose and name be one,
Let us build upon the Father's treasures
We are his delight and joy

Rejoice my beloved
I shall give you life anew
Loneliness shall vanish away
You shall shine with beams of joy

Rejoice my beloved
The future will govern my expression of love,

When your heart is enlarged, I shall fill with love,
I shall pour it out as the rain from heaven,
Tomorrow's love, today hasn't seen.

Rejoice my beloved;
I have been tempted to forget thee
I am my father's beloved,
Obey him precious one
He shall keep us together

Rejoice my beloved;
Joy hast flushed o'er my soul,
I have received love and duly respect,
Time shall be ruled by thee,
Thy soul shall be rewarded with joy.

Rejoice my beloved
In trouble I'll not forsake thee,
Though wounded, I shall protect thee,
The bewitched shall have to flee,
I am thy love, I am thy keeper,

Rejoice my beloved;
I have lifted your burdens,
The joy of life has beautified thee.
I have saved you from the wolf in sheep-clothing.
Through thought's I shall protect thee

Rejoice my beloved,
My love brought you from the wilderness,
My father's love hast blessed you,
In patience I have taught you,
Freely receiving, I freely give,

Rejoice my beloved,
I am your joy in tomorrow,
I am the peace of your seasons,
I am the fulfilling of your happiness,
Rejoice, Rejoice, Rejoice, my beloved.

(Song)

We Shall Build God's House

1969

We shall build
We shall build the house of the Lord
For the time is now appointed

We shall build
We shall build the house of the Lord
We the workers are anointed
To build the house of the Lord
To build the house of the Lord

They shall come from the east and west
From the north and the south
There shall arise a great people
In the name of Jehovah, Jehovah, Jehovah

We shall build his temple with haste
There is no time to waste
This hour and this place
Build now the house of the Lord
Build now the house of the Lord

Reign With Him

One of these mornings,
You'll look for me and I'll be gone
I'm going to heaven, I'll have nothing to do
But rule in God's heavens all day

I'll meet my father, my mother will be there too
I'll do nothing, nothing, but sing and praise
But when He says well done, my race on earth will be run
Join hands together and rule in God's heaven all day

Hear me when I cry
Walk by my side
Hold my hand when the going gets tough
I need you to be my guide

Everyday will be Sunday the Sabbath will have no end
We'll sing & praise.
All our days
We will rule
From God's heaven always.

Christian Love slave

I will always be your love slave
    Loving only you,
You will always be my master
    With tender love so true

A thousand tons of silver,
    A million tons of gold,
Could never bring me happiness,
    If your love would grow cold.

I will always be your love slave.
    Coming whenever you call.
Hoping one day to stay forever,
    And be your all in all.

No one could ever thrill my heart
    That special way you do
No I could not begin to tell
    The joy that surges through
Sweet, Jesus, I love you.

Doorkeeper

Be a doorkeeper
Not in the traditional way
Be a doorkeeper
Hear what the Lord has to say

The Lord is going in and out
He doesn't leave his house in doubt
He tells us what he wants us to do
Leaves it with us to carry it through

Most times housekeepers
Are left with full command
Sometimes doorkeepers
Must take a holy stand

Behold I stand at the door and knock
Certainly this is the Lord's remarks
If you will dare to let him in
He will cleanse your life from sin
Be a doorkeeper not in the traditional way
Be a doorkeeper hear what the spirit doth say

Don't just usher the saints of God
Usher also His word
Speak it lively, boldly, fervently
Just as your heart has heard

Our heart is the door
The knocking is the word
If any man will open, then he has heard
If any is closed on his accord
Then he rejects and turn away the Lord

We surely should be examples today
We stand by the door, "The Way"
Positions only play the part
That God has put in each man heart

Ushers do arise today
Be examples and do display
If you've never thought of this before
Think of your heart as the door

Be the keepers of your heart
Let the Word of God have it's start
The knocking is the word
Let him in
Whatever your ministry
I shall ascend
The spirit and the word agree

Missionary

Abraham father of the Jew
Abraham father of Islam too
Noah, the father of Ham, Japeth and Shem
Noah's wife the mother of all of them

Noah, his wife, whose name is not given
Their three sons and wives beget all the living
One earth, one society of men
Populated the earth once again

Nimrod led them all to sin
Confusion of language and blood kin
They then formed different clans
To dwell with the ones they did understand

Some begin to call it race
They then all moved to a different place
Atmospheric pressure did change their face
That migration became their base

Love and health found in blacks
Strength and military might
Humor and entertainment
Muscular size from midget to giant

Dare devils and men of war
Killing and taking what they saw
Justifying it all by law
Greed, greed, inside did gnaw

Blue eyes, blond hair, and skin so fair
No willingness to give or share
Did not just slow a man down
Killed and laid them all in the ground

Through Abraham God gave a man
To rule this earth by heavens plan
To live together in harmony and peace
To live together successfully.

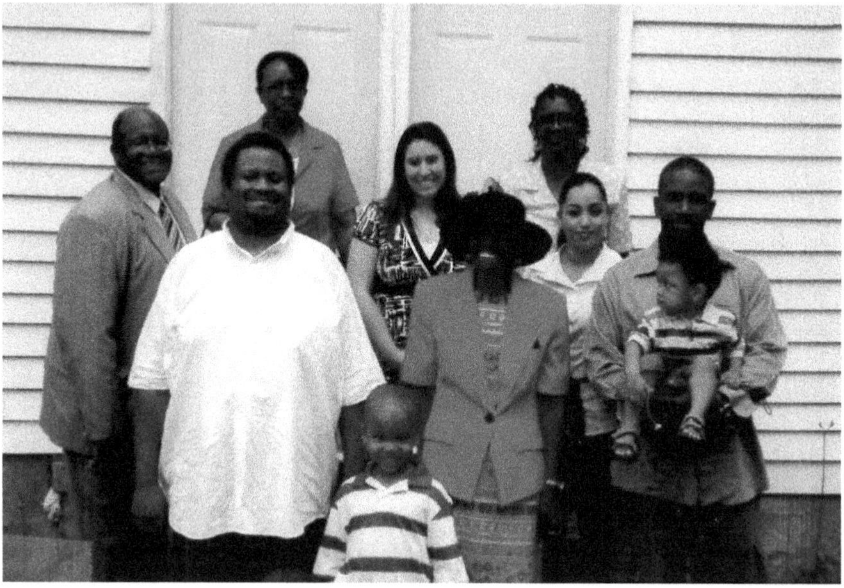

History
In
Poetry

> *"History will be kind to me,*
> *For I intend to write it"*
>
> - Winston S. Churchill

Memories Of Our Barn

1963

Still, silent, empty,
Our barn now stands alone
nothing to fill the empty space.
as it was when I was home
no one to care for it as once we did
when our life was young and gay.
for now. mother is old, her children are grown
and papa has passed away.

So now the barn is deserted
and it stands alone
and the farm place is now but a shack
the barn soon will be the same
cause no ones coming back

My older brothers are married, my sisters are too
I was the youngest child, and last at the farm to toil,
I guess that's why it hurts me the most
to see the old place go to spoils.

As I stand here now looking at the weather beaten boards
which could do with three coats of paints or more.
It makes me want to build again
and tent the place like I helped do before
A lot of money it would take to build the homestead again
for looking over the landscape far as I can see
The barn is the only building that steadily stands
But even seeing this brings joy to me.

Frolly Gee

My name is Frolly Gee
    I've won a victory,
I'm now a hero in the
    Army of Nero
A wealthy man is he.

My name is Frolly Gee
    Wont you join me in tea
Alcohol, is, much too strong.
    So a tea drinker is me.
My name is Frolly Gee.

My name is Frolly Gee
    I'm as busy as a bumble bee
You'd better do it right
    In my eyesight, or else
I'll certainly see
    A bright young lad is Frolly Gee

Chill Man Chill

(4-8-96)

Hey, my brother acting up over there
What's that I hear coming from your mouth,
Did I hear you curse and swear?
Did I hear you using profanity
In the class, in the streets, in the home
Did I hear your tongue making sounds with your mouth
that will bring you only scorn?
Chill, brother chill!!

Sit down black brother in the teacher's classroom
Don't get loud cause I know that you're there
Take your hands off that girl while she's in the classroom
Stop feeling on her body, disgracing her everywhere
Use your head my brother, and not your hands
Cause I know its going on up there
Respect that teacher in the classroom, my brother
Or else you don't have a prayer
Chill, brother chill

Don't show your behind my brother, in the street
A baby's behind is the only one that's bare
Pick up your pants my brother from your knees and feet
The world knows you've got something down there
Don't prostitute, my brother, what you do so well
Let it wait, let it ride, let it hide
Have something my brother that the world hasn't seen
To the world let it be a surprise
Chill brother, chill

If she's easy don't you be the one who tries to please her
You're the sunrising and you're the sunsetting
If you don't be giving, she can't begetting
Are you gonna be a father while you're a teenager
To control in life, don't be a stranger
You were born to be a-leader and leader you are
Don't lead others to playing chicken with your car
Don't lead others to be a clown in school
Don't lead others to break the golden rule
Chill my brother, chill
Stay in church, stay in school
Chill my brother, chill

Columbus

"You know, there must be man,
    In a far and distant land."
"Somewhere far across the sea
    Ambitious and happy like you and me."

There must be life,
    In some fashion or form.
Where crops are harvested
    And children are born.

The earth is round
    This I do know.
For friends of mine,
    Have proved it so,

The earth is round,
    It's round like a sphere,
And there is land.
    Elsewhere than here.

It takes a man to find the way
    Who fears not the danger, the ocean display
Who will go on and on weeks after weeks
    To discover at last that which he seeks.

What is Black

April 1991

Black is more than being born
With course kinky hair

Black is more than a lost people
Trying to find somewhere

Black is more than a light so bright
It puts a shine through thickened tar

Black is more than loving your children
All people of the world

Black is more than having the answers
Which the world will never hurl

Black is more than suffering the cause
The Governments upon your shoulders

Black is more than loving others
Slavemasters, cruel and less Godlier

Black is more than crack cocaine
Booz or aphrodisiacs

Black is more than education
Just to serve and carry the facts

Black is more than the solid mind
Egoes do come and go

Black is more than health and strength
Being rich or being poor

Black is, smothering disgrace
Which would destroy the world

Black is, being a vehicle
With detour on every sign

Black is being in prison
Until an assigned time

Black is not having enough
Still, being supplied with more

Black is knowing you have no money
Yet going to the store

Black is hating the master who made you slave

Black is loving the person till he gets saved

Black is more than words can ever express
Black is what?
Take a guess

Deception

(1974)

    Navy annex loading dock
Sitting on a skid with an open box
    Brochures within was such a shock
To be found at a government stop

    The "Rightness of Whiteness"
Was what I read
    Contents imbedded in my head
To this day have never fled
    Understanding of societal cultural ed.
United States white children were fed

    Distorted biblical truths of Almighty God
Delivered to white children was a fraud
    By parents, by clergy, by teachers too
Artistic images know to be untrue
    Spread throughout the entire world
Distortions to create racism
    A superior mind-set was given
By evangelical Americans and Europeans
    Deception to a world of human beings

Thank You Toussaint

5/20/1743-4/7/1803

    You helped America grow
Though you did not know
    Your survival in the land of Haiti
Forced Napoleon to spend greatly
    He sold to America in a state of emergency
We know it as the Missouri Treaty

    Your warfare ability
Was quite a sight to see
    Out-doing Italian nobility
You forced respect to keep all free
    Like a cat trying to catch a 'mouse
You proved that he was in your house

The native of Haiti was all black
    Napoleon's army skilled and white
Did not expect to meet psychology
    From the looks of those seen in Haiti
To whom God gave ability
    Never was hereditary

Freedom

(1/7/2019)

    Liberty liberty you're close to me
Closer than what you used to be
    When Jim Crowe had victory
Filled us with fear and disharmony

    I see our statue in my mind
A flaming torch is hard to find
    Barely lit in this evil time
When justice is no longer blind

Our freedoms, our freedoms are at stake
Escalating is the crime rate
    A land assigned by Almighty God
To be his staff, to be his rod

    Fight to keep the flame bright
Fight to keep it in your sight
    Fight with all your mental might
Fight, fight, fight

Pro-Lynched

From North Carolina
He cross the state line
To harvest tobacco was not a crime
To work each day at the
Tobacco barn
Making eyes and touching
Mesmerized by charm
One handsome guy two hot babes
Played a game that could have
Created a grave.
The boy knew well
The girls did not
He could have been killed
had he been caught

So when girls wanted to make it public
The black had been allowed what the white could only covet
The black boy would not agree
Knowing he could be hung from a tree
Would not own up to what they had done

Aware of southern persecution
for being carefree with white girls
Was not allowed in the southern world

He shyed away from the friendship offered
Warned of what could have occurred
White women affections had to be benched
Lest some black man would be lynched
Based on rules of KKK
Most black men knew how to play.
Hopeful for change to come someday.
Praying for God to take KKK away.

Who Am I?

10-1988

Who am I
I am the Father of Homosapien
The first of all mankind

Who am I
I am called the Original Man
The image of God in Adam shines

Who am I
I am rooted from the Ethiopian
The wife of Moses being one

Who am I
I am the Pharaohs of Egypt Land
The wife of Joseph, mother of, Ephraim and Manasseh

Who am I
I am the backbone of civilization
In math and music I excelled

Who am I
I am Nimrod; the Father of the Nation
The Tower of Babel my creation

I am the essence of every man
Medicine and Science are mine

Who am I
I am the architect of the Pyramids
The wisdom of the world

Who am I
I am the wealthy possessor of goldmines
Queen of Sheba gave them to Solomon

Who am I
I am the teacher of Plato
Africa is my epotiem

Who am I
I am a man whose skin is black
With thick lips I sing my songs

Who am I
I am the muscle and sinew of Hercules
Even my nose is muscle toned

Who am I
I am gentle, loving and kind
You made me a tortured slave, yet I nursed your young

Who am I
I am popcorn air of black and brown
You know me as Negro

Who am I
I am compassion, who carried The Cross
When Jesus could not go

Who am I
I am Cleopatra of Julius Caesar
And Mark Anthony too

Who am I
I am you
Black, Colored or White
You came from me you will go back
Black black, fair black, and light black

One world, one people, in God's sight.

Moving Ahead

Rap on brother
If you're black, you're black
Don't be ashamed if your skin ain't white
Rap on brother
Cause it's alright

Rap on brother
Rap on for your cause
You've got a message
You've seen the flaws
Rap on brother
Rap on for your cause

Just keep on pushin
Can't stop now
A better day's a-coming
Someway somehow

Right on brother
Rap strong to the white
Keep on pushin
Don't stop and go back
A better way's a-coming
Somehow, someday
When black kids and white kids
Together will play

Contributus

1972

In this writing we see a formula of contributions for mankind
To see, to speak, to be, to feel, to show and to inscribe.

Black Man see it!!
See what God wants you to see
See how creative are we,
See that man should not have to plea
To get justice and equality,
And when they take away your eyes
And they will
Let your spirit be your guide
Black Man, see it!!

Black Man say it!!
Get down on your knees and pray it
Say it to give all mankind strength
Say it to those you're up against
Say it cause your tongue don't pay no rent
Black Man say it!!

Black Man be it!!
Be it because it's of God and good
Be it because you know you should
Be it that it might be understood
You ain't no bum, you ain't no hood
Black Man be it, then be it good.

Black Man feel it!!
Don't be scared cause you know you didn't steal it
Feel it cause it's real, it's earthly, it's true

Black Man feel it,... Cause it's me, it's you
If that's all that you can do
Black Man feel it!!

Black Man show it!!
Forget about yourself lest your hatred blow it
Like a lawnmower cut it down and mow it
Black Man show it!!
Show it you're a Duke, a Prince, a President, a King
You've got the ability to rule and reign
Show it, so the world can live in peace again
Black Man show it!!

Black Man inscribe it!!
Don't let historians later hide it
Inscribe it in the public news
Inscribe it over the T.V. tubes
Inscribe it in your rapp, gospels, jazz and blues
Black Man inscribe it
Inscribe it in a way only Geniuses can
Inscribe it so the world will know your span
Inscribe it as the most intelligent christian man
Black Man inscribe it!!

Colors

by Nathan Carmichael
Nathan Carmichael a third grader in 1990 wrote these words

Black the color of the people
White the color of the snow
Indian the color,
I don't know

I Tell You A Truth

5/92

An Asian-American speaks to an Afro-American about the distorted image the white society presents and supports in America. -Part truth -Part lie

I tell you a truth
Policeman...for white society
Policeman not for you
Policeman not for me
Policeman not for justice and law
As they do often say
Policeman for caucasian
The rest of us are prey.

I tell you a truth
Freedom... for white society
Freedom not for you
Freedom not for me
Freedom first- class citizen
Here in U.S.A
Freedom, liberty and happiness
Don't come the second-class way

I tell you a truth
Justice... For white society
Justice not for you
Justice not for me
Justice not color blind
Though eyes be covered by cloth

Justice stored way in closet
And we are not the moth

I tell you a truth
Christian.... For white society
Christian not for you
Christian not for me
Christian white as Jesus Christ
Though he was a dark skinned Jew
No blond hair, no eyes of blue
Adam and God,... all white too.

I tell you a truth
Truth...for white society
Truth not for you
Truth not for me
Truth not to cover itself, In color taints of hue
According to the white man
Truth comes not from me of mine
Truth comes not from blacks like you
Truth not even come from the Jew

Now I tell a little white lie
Blackman, no good except to die
Stealing and killing what he do best
As long as he lives, society no rest
He no honor... His family no crest
He do no good when take a test
Blackman, all should be in jail
Blackman, all go down to hell

White man told me all my time
Blackman no Plato, Blackman no Einstein
He no plus mankind

He make baby illegitimately
He no work... He lazy
White man taught me, ask him why
Why I tell a little white lie
If I tell a pure whole truth
I like Blackman also die
I tell you a truth
White truth is lie.

Proud to be Black

10/91

I was born
Just like you
In this country
Told I could be equal
Proud to be black

I've got good thoughts
About man and nature
To better mankind
In this earth
Proud to be black

I attended schools
Sixteen long years plus
Training my mind
To think the thoughts to better myself
Proud to be black

I drink the water
From a one source system
When I'm thirsty
To quench that natural salt-based thirst
Proud to be black

I can walk down a street
In your neighborhood
And be thrown in jail
Because you thought I shouldn't be there
Proud to be black

I can apply for a job
The same time as you
More qualified
And be turned down
Proud to be black

I can fight in wars
To protect the land I love
First to shed my blood
First to loose my life
To be denied opportunity
Proud to be black

When I'm deceased
My mortal remains cannot be buried
In any cemetery of my choice
Proud to be black

I shall become stronger
I shall overcome
I shall survive
I shall conquer my feats
Amidst adversity
Proud to be black

I shall rule the public
Though you say my brains too weak
Mayors, congressmen, presidents and staff
Criticized, threatened, and put to death
I'll succeed on the proven path
Jehovah, Jesus, and our ancestors Left
Proud to be black.

Value of a Man

I saw men selling a hog one day
The worth of the hog was in what it did weigh
Another man took a cow to a county fair
It was graded by its built, its teeth, and color of its hair
A woman gave birth to a bastered child
Put it up for adoption because its father was
was ugly, brutal, and wild
She judged it to be like its natural clan, but tell
me can this be the value of a man
When I look at a man can I see his soul, when
I look at a man can I tell his goal
Can I see the spirit of life, which churns
within, when I look at a man can I see his spleen.

The value of a man is not in the way he looks
Not in the educational courses he took
The value of a man is not in his speech
Nor in the type of people he daily meet.
The value of a man is not in his size.
His half type, nor the color of his eyes

You cannot even begin
To determine man's value by the color of his skin
These are just superficial things
To protect the true being which dwells within.

The value of a man is in the deeds he does
His innate ability to show true love.
The values of a man is in the discipline of the mind.
How he rules and governs within his time.
The value of a man is in the speaking of words
But in response to what he has heard

Blackman, Negro, or Colored Boy

That Blackman's gonna take his stand
    Ain't bout to run from no Klu Klux Klan
First He'd die on his peice of land
    Foe they rob him for being a man

Ain't got much just a color that hated
    A wife, son and daughter that's underated
Fer this nobody was created
    A fine good woman can't even be a lady

So he with skin as black as tar
That's gonna be the same today, tomorrow
Till his Jesus call him away
He can't change this black clay

The negro didn't know where to go
He was hued, smart, weak and poor
He was an educated stool
Who was cheated in school
He was told you be good
You keep cool
Maybe you've got something we can use

He showed he was good
He kept cool
Still he didn't rule
He would squeal on his mother
To save his own skin
Just to be in with white men

The colored boy was a paper doll toy
He never grew older he just slayed a boy
Being a boy was his reward
He labored and worked his whole life hard
Just to measure up to be a boy

He did what he was told
No matter the times he was sold
From this master to that
He'd labour and sweat
Won't nothing at all he could get
Except soakin wet
And never got annoyed
Cause he was a toy
Just a paper-toy colored boy

Yes sir, yes maam
Don't talk back to white folks Sam
You mind your manners
Cause we been good to you
Get that rag, here, shine my shoe
Feed my dog Sam, when they are through
Give your family what they are due

Just a colored paper doll toy
At 65 he was still a boy
He got to be an uncle
If he didn't grumble,
Forgot the freedom he had in the jungle
Serve two generations without a stumble
At seventy or so
He'd become an uncle

Glutton's Revival

All of a sudden
I've seen the light
I'm gonna change my appetite

Collard greens
You ain't my thing
I've sophisticated
From these stewed t'matos

Cornbread fried
You done an died
Cause I'm gonna push
You all aside

All of a sudden
I've seen the light
I'm gonna change my appetite

Macaroni and cheese
All you soul faces
On my table
Dees here days

Casseroles, Lord bless my soul
Can't afford to let them get cold
That cracklin salads
That dressing called French
Me and them just got to commence
All of a sudden I've seen the light
I'm gonna change my appetite

Jim Beckwourth

His mother black, his father white
Broke the law in Virginia's sight
Born into slavery and Jim Crowe
Becwourth had no place to go in 1824
Joined a party going west began for him his first test
A mountain man, fur trapper an Indian chief
Getting away from American slavery
Helped the white man go safely west
By a route called Beckwourth Pass
This black man fought slavery and did win
To everyman he was his kin
The white man's treaty they did resend
So he died fighting with the Indians.

Don't You Know Me

1989

The white man sought us out of a greedful, destructive, curiosity, to get to know us. He needed to master us to satisfy his greed therefore he cheated himself of knowing who we really are.

Don't y'know, don't y'know
Don't y'know who I am?
I'm not your left over food
I'm not your candid yams.
I'm not some simple freak who don't belong
I'm not some robot minsteral
To dance to your songs

Don't y'know, don't y'know
Don't y'know where I'm at
I'm not lower than the flea
I'm not smaller than the gnat
I'm not your low life animal
??? your creepy insect
??? homosapien man
??? due respect

You put me in a cage
You couldn't keep me there
You gave me a phony deal
A phony freedom share
I, who was once your fantasy
Now, I'm your nightmare
Amidst your hysterical ways
You lost all love and care
Are you really that bare??

You can never train the creature
If you never love and share
You can never soothe the savage
Be it squirrel or grizzly bear
Don't you know, I'm rare,
The style of my trousers
You're too lofty to wear
Don't you know, don't you know
Don't you know we pair

Don't y'know our nursing mother
She nursed a baby on each breast
One, a child of her womb
One, was of her master's home
Feeding her blood made into milk
From her tortured body
Scared by the whip
Don't you know me now, I'm kinship

Bill Pickett

Cowboy Bill Pickett
    Some people thought he witched it
He roped those cattle fast and easy
    Like a magician performing a trick

He mastered cows like no other
    He invented bulldogging
His rugged body took pain and torture
    The cows all from him, took a flogging

"Kings of Cowboys"
    His earned title
No Hollywood involved
    His motions, smooth as a bell ringing

Greatest on the rodeo stand
    Born when a blackman
Wasn't spit on the ground
    Bill Pickett made a worldwide sound
"Greatest Cowboy of the Day"

Escape

(1969)

From all of life that puzzles me,
I'm escaping to find myself,
To rid my mind of inqusition,
and let soberance of mind become my staff.

I ran fast to the shaded tree,
To escape from the shadow that followed me,
I only hid it from my stare and later
I found out ... it was still there

I ran to the fast, cool, flowing beach,
To escape from all this scorching heat.
I found myself again in sweat.
When I returned home where I was first at

I tried to escape from the marching wars,
Because I disapproved of the national laws
This left me again in thought
I could not escape as I had sought

I tried to escape from life's misery,
To become happy joyful and full of glee
I found even this I could not do
I was to misery as paper is to glue

I've tried it in every way, I see
But I cannot become a successful escapee
I tried to escape from the girls untrue
And found myself stuck with an old shoe.

I guess to escape would be the wrong thing to do
I guess I should stay and fight it through
You see .... I'm puzzled as, whether run or stay
To fight .... or to seek "escape!"

Episode of the Mind
1969

Why can't we understand
The principles which govern
The life of man
The earth
      the sun
           the sky
The answers to the reasons why.

What causes the carefree birds to sing?
What makes the rays of the sun beam?
What makes the sky
Cloudy or fair?
Or the wind to tangle a young girls' hair?
What is judgement and how is it known?
Where is beauty and how is it shown?
Who are the haters, who destroy mankind?
Where is the love we seek to find?

Where is wisdom
So timid and shy
Always escaping the human eye
And why the struggle of the mind
To give insight to the culturally blind.

Scientific inventions forever increasing
Problems of man never ceasing
Moral virtue at a rapid decline
Principles once learned
Now left behind.

These are the episodes of the mind
These are the episodes of the mind

George Washington Carver
Peanut man, peanut man
How did you think, how did you stand
What loving person whose skin was white
Did not treat you as a no good black

You loved the south, you loved it's reason
The growth of plants from season to season
You made discoveries for all mankind
From the peanut and the sweet potato vine
You invented a milk, foods and soap
The poor was fed, the farmer had hope

When given a chance though born a slave
A difference to the world was made
scientist, scholar, inventor, too
A Christian soldier his whole life through.

Parenthood

Father and Mother together came
Not just for me

Father and Mother gave me life
To live eternally

Father and Mother gave
Everything they had to give
Throughout their life
Their purpose was that I might live

They showed me how to walk
They showed me how to talk
They showed me how to laugh and cry
To say hello and never ever goodby

They showed me how to love
When times are good
When times are bad

They showed me how give
When all are happy
When all are sad

They showed me how to struggle
When storms of life do come
How to endure in troubled times
And never become undone

Father and Mother
Combined in all their children
Are one.

Vision

No matter how bad
Hard times are
They're not as bad
As they seem
As long as there's someone
With a sense of humor
And a workable
Encompassing dream

A Man

Played as a child I have for so long
Now is the time to come on strong
Release myself from binding games
From stunts that will never bring fame
To come alive to take my stand
And show the world I AM A MAN

The tears of yesterday must go
The joy of today must swiftly flow
The thoughts of what tomorrow can be
With the help of people like you and me
Men must stand in unity

Must I forever be called son
Does my growth indicate I am one
Must I be led by someones hands
Not grown enough to give commands
Or shall I show I have a plan
Let the world know I AM A MAN

Branching from what I used to be
I now have reached maturity
Yet still, there's a long way to go
So many ideas I must show

That people may see
That people may know
Here is a man
A child no more

Dr. Charles Drew

Charles Drew you knew
Not because your skin was white
Charles Drew you knew
Not because your race was black

You knew because God is one
He made the moon He made the sun
He made the Jew though they be few
You knew because God made you

You knew the blood of all men was one
Because you believed God's only son
You saved millions of lives and saving still
The truth of blood that all men spill
And yet because your race was black
And prejudice separated black and white
You needed blood and could not be treated
Because your truth by all was not heeded
Because of evil men your life depleted.

My Family

1975

Jacob Bowens I to James Bowens II, III, IV-IX
1850 to present

Many a seed hast been sown
This family tree has grown and grown
Planted in the days of old
When slaves were still being sold
By ancestors hast been foretold

In the time when slaves were still
A people was labeled Free Ishel
Also called Croatans
After called Indians in this land

So was Jacob Bowens the first
One of many sons to be
From the town of Bolton N.C.
The founding father of this family

A son was born whose name was James
Highly honoring his mother's name
Found a Francis and she was game
Husband and wife they became
We today are their remains
Fashioned and moulded from their frames
Seventh and more generations of the Bowens name

You are my flesh
You are my soul
You are my family

Blood of my blood
Seed of my seed
Genes of my family tree
You are my mother
You are my father
You are my grand
My great, great
And great great great

My uncles my aunts
Neices and nephews
My cousins by the slew

You are that drop of rain
Which became a puddle
A pond, a stream, a river, a sea

In tissue, in fiber we are the same
I am you and you are me
We are geneology

Men, women and children
Ruler to be of this earth
Queens and kings
Of different things
Forgetting not our birth.

We are one of many
Families of the land
Struggling to not forget
We are all one clan.

Good Father, My Father

by Nathan Carmichael

Leading me and guiding me
Showing me the way
You only want the best for me
So you teach me each day
Lecturing and disciplining
Teaching and explaining
You fit the description of a good father
You fit the description of my father

You mold and shape me to be the best I can be
To follow your footsteps
To be greater than thee
You encourage me to reach for my dreams
You show me that they are actually closer than they seem
You check up on me during the night
You come to see if everything is all right
You fit the description of a good father
You fit the description of my father

You enlighten me to the truth
You enlighten me to Christ
So I myself will not have to pay the ultimate price
You show me the right way
Always from day to day
You truly fit the description of a good father
You truly fit the description of my father

P.S. 　　　　　Thank you father for being a good father
(Poem Script) Not like some fathers who don't even bother
　　　　　　　But you my friend you are the prime example
　　　　　　　of a good father
　　　　　　　I wrote these special words in this special way
　　　　　　　For you my good father on this father's day

Share Cropper Prayer WFC

1860's-1960's

    Jesus Jesus take me home
Ain't did no wrong
    I'm just a sharecropper
with a song
    Only thing to me belong

    Mr Tom's place sho ain't mine
Get te thinkin that way some time
    I ain't nutin but a slave
Sharecropper called, these here days

    That ol'mule Mr Tom owns
Treated better then my bones
    feels like he owns me too
Whatever he say I gotta do

    He rapes my wife when I'm in the fields
A high yellow child his seed yields
    Another mouth I gotta feed
With the ration he gives my family and me
    And to get dat I had to plea
Jesus Jesus take me home

Abolitionist

Thanks to Abolition
Benjamin Lay and John Brown
Thanks to Abolition
Christopher Sower Sowed Germantown

All Americans are great Americans
A place for humanity's blend
Every Christian is an equal Christian
Brothers and sisters forgiven of sin

Free to breathe, free to cry
Free to laugh, free to sigh
Free of cultures all gone by
Free to oneness beneath the sky
Jew, Greek, rich, poor, black and white are we
One people embracing Christianity
Free to love, free to marry

Barack Obama

BARACK OBAMA, BARACK OBAMA
IN 2008 A PRESIDENTIAL DRAMA
A SHINING LIGHT FOR WORLDWIDE CHANGE
A BLESSING OF WISDOM, EVEN HIS NAME

A HANDSOME MAN, AN ELOQUENT SPEAKER
A RADICAL FORCE, A PRESIDENTIAL SEEKER
A MIND OF VISION, OF CLARITY, OF DEPT
A TRUST TO THE NATION'S CONSTITUTIONAL MAP

SO LONG AWAITED, NOW HOPE APPEARING
A LEGAL GENIUS, A SOCIAL SHEARING
A CLARITY TO WHAT WE SAID WE ARE
A SURGEON TO REMOVE A NATIONAL SCAR

A SENATOR, A HUSBAND, A LOVING FATHER
A FAITHFUL MAN, BARACK OBAMA
A NATIONAL TREASURE FROM ILLINOIS
TO LEAD THIS GREAT NATION FORWARD
    A CERTIFIED RECONIZED WORLDWIDE REWARD
    BARACK OBAMA BARACK OBAMA

From Hawaii

Eight pounds two ounces of pure joy
Arrived in Hawaii in the form of a boy
A little shy a little coy
The world received a precious reward

The man we know the icon we carved
The messenger we all prayed for
Not a genie in a jar
A flesh and blood deliverer

The state of Hawaii,
His place to be
Amid racial diversity
The stage was set for victory
On the landscape of creativity

Like two volcanic craters
This child would be a revelator
Mild and calm his outward appearance
But resilient when he is warried against

My Grandson

My grandson, my pride and joy
Although his skin, is not white
My grandson, a little boy
Kind, generous, always polite

My grandson, on my shoulders he will sit
His vision will not be impaired
He will see when other will not
And what he does see it will be shared

My grandson, a statuesque growth of mankind
He will repair, he will bring together
He will remove prejudicial actions
He will formulate what other shatter

My thoughts, my hopes, for me and mine
In my grandson will shine
In place him on shoulder strong
My grandson, above king kamehamehas' throne
To my grandson royalty, belongs

Just A Man

Our president-elect
He is afro-american
Well, isn't he just a man

Our president-elect
He is the first of his racial clan
Well, isn't he just a man

Our president-elect
He did not faint when he did stand
Well isn't that like a man

Our president-elect
Heard the nation's great demand
Well, isn't he just a man

Our president-elect
Delivered minds from cultural quick sand
Well, isn't he just a man

Homo sapien
A man
Part caucasian
A man
Mentally cognizant
A man
Enforcing a master plan
A man

He was, he is, ever so grand
Barack Obama
He is just a man

Help him help him
All you can
He maybe a genius
He is just a man
The man we chose to give
Your man, our man, command world's authoritarian
Conductor of the human band
Grammatical, handsome, earthian
Barack Obama is just a man

In Time

*From Fredrick Douglas to Hiram Revels
to Martin Luther King, Statesmen,
Orators, Politicians Voices full of
inspiration Minds to save a troubled
nation*
    Was beard in time

*Four hundred years our nation preparing
Two strong cultures continually sharing
Praying for a day, an instance bearing
A son, a man, to be so daring*
    Arrived in time

*Praises, shouts of adulation
Hearts filled with ancient sensations
Eyes once dimmed, now given vision
Humanity crowned, a racial incision*
    He stood up in time

Hall To The Chief

O'Great one of pure logic
    We hall you
    O'Needed one of common sense
    We hall you
    O'Master of the constitution
    We hall you
    O'Doctor of social healing
    We hall you

    We hall you because of
    The God who sent you
    We hall you because of
    The creator who formed you
    We hall you because
    You heard and obeyed
    Pres. Barack O'Bama
    We hall you
    We hall you because of
    Christ who taught you

Paid the price on calvary and bought you
    Gave you new life to live again
    President O'Bama
    We hall you.

White House Days

As I recall the white house
    Each morning signing in
    Standing before the officers desk
    At the executive office building
A Little lady getting out of a mercedes benz
    With a large shopping bag in her hand
    Who was allowed to sat in the executive foyer
    From day to day with no special plan

    The small quaint library to which I was sent
    After 30 years was closing down
    Due to the librarian retirement
    Not knowing from which agency
    Her checks were going to come
    Her presidential appointment
    Had long been forgotten

    Surreal, according to todays standards
    Of such increased securities
    Since the ninthteen seventies

    Boxes and boxes of books I recall
    From floor to ceiling from wall to wall
    Her special collection of caystal cats
    By no means would she let me forget

Vice president Rockerfeller
    Shaking everyones' hand
    Appreciative of the assignment
    With president Ford it had began

Most Moral President

In 1977 Jesus sent
To Washington D.C. as President
From the state of Georgia, he did come
A spiritual job had to be done

He could not preach right or wrong
The Holy Bible did not belong
Separation of church and state
Did not allow the teaching in the White House gates.

First a teacher for Jesus Christ
A leader of men in military life
Our 39th President he became
Keeping the faith of Christ's fame

He lived the life others just talked
His Christian belief was his Christian walk
He gave honor to Christianity
Did not compromise because of presidency
President Carter,
A true believer and christian
Made many changes from the status-quo
To restrict office fratinizing.
Or I suppose it so.
White House days
1977 3 or 4 decades ago.

Barry/Barack

Barry draws pictures in the mind
To think of sweetness the natural kind
Cranberry, blueberry, cherry pies
The mouth and palate can appetize

Birds of the air on berries feast
Domesticated and even wild beast
The thoughts of Barry creates good taste
Someone to be in a special place

Barack, solid as a rock
Can be trusted, does not mock
Not easily crushed, a friend of friends
He'll be right there until the end

Barack, uncommon as it sounds
Identifies with a crown
A king, a shiek, a medicine man
Qualified to take a stand
A man full of good plans

In My Dreams

I've seen you my father
    In my dreams
I've talked to you, my father
    In my dreams
So real, so real, so real it seemed
      Yet it was then in my dreams

You reached out
    Through a dream it seems
Because your love
    Was so extreme
Your love for me
    It was not a dream

In my mother, and your heart too
    A love created
My life brand new
    Your vision and her's a society
Was born again
    Embodied in me

I love you my father
    Tis not a dream
I felt your joy, I felt your pain
    Now more than feelings still remain
For in life's stream
    You are real, more than a dream

So glad I knew you your frame
    and size
So glad I saw you the light in
    your eyes

So glad I watched you breathing
    breath
So glad I touched you before you left
    So glad I heard your oral
expressions
    It filled my life
    It left no guessing

I Remember You

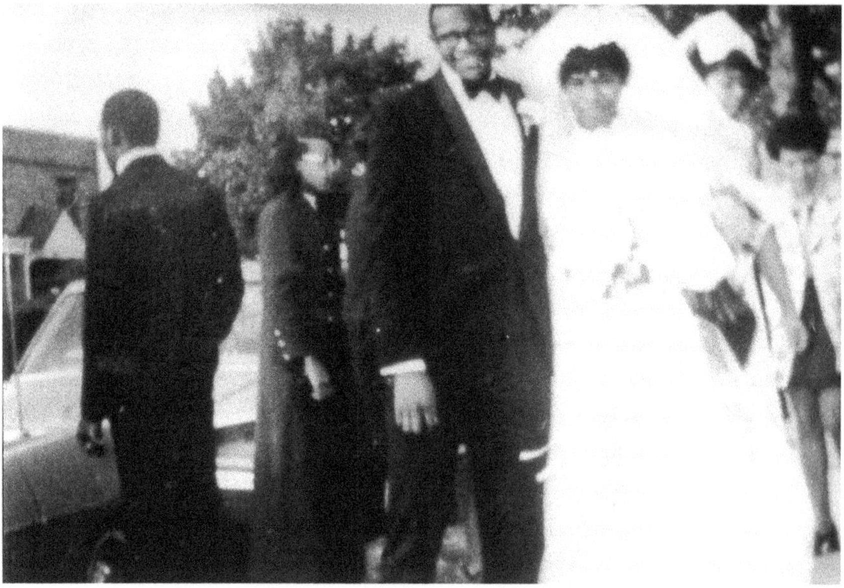

Appreciation

Thank you Uncle Winston
For always being kind
To see your face, to hear your voice
Brings to me peace of mind

Thank you Uncle Winston
For being in God's plan
Your choice to just be you
Makes you a special man

Your smile is yours alone
It's like a calm, soothing song
Your voice is never in a hurry
Yet still I know
I know sometimes, even you worry

Your inner strength is your control
Giving you a shining role
To which you've been a mighty man
Still, now, you boldly stand.

You are a star, a shinning star
This light of yours has shone so far
You're built with a lot of integrity
So now, you be as you be

Thank you, for sharing your life with me
You've not been selfish to any degree
In my book you're highly esteemed
Uncle Willie Winston McLean

A Gift

Dedicated to Doris Lee Carmichael-Williams
11/1945-5-1993

THE MASTER OF ALL CREATIONS
SAW A NEED ON EARTH ONE DAY
HE SENT A WILLING SERVANT
TO NURSE OUR PAIN AWAY

THE HOME OF JOHN WILLIE AND GLADYS
WAS VISITED WITH LOVE
A NEW MEMBER TO THE FAMILY
FROM THE FATHER UP ABOVE

SHE WAS QUITE AND TEMPERATE
VERY INTELLIGENT WAS SHE
NEVER DID SHE BOAST OR FLAUNT IT
AS SUPERIORITY

PERFORMING ALL HER DUTIES
AT HOME, WORK, SCHOOL AS WELL
HER PHILOSOPHY WAS SIMPLE
"DO WHAT YOU HAVE TO DO"

FROM HIGH SCHOOL TO NURSING
TO A FAMILY OF TENDER LOVE
SHE SHARED HER GIFT OF LIFE
WITH SMILES, WITH TEARS, WITH HUGS

NOT PERFECT, YET GIVING US PERFECTION
NOT WHOLE, YET MAKING OTHERS COMPLETE
NO GODDESS, YET GIVING US HER GUIDANCE
NO PRIESTESS, YET HELPING US TO SEE

HER ROLE AS WIFE, MOTHER, AND HEALER
WAS SERIOUS TO THE END
NOW, HER ROLE TO THE HEAVENLY FATHER
WILL FOREVER ASCEND
SHE WILL NURSE MANY FROM THE TREE OF LIFE
WHEN HER NEW POSITION BEGINS.

Just A Mortal Man

In Memories of Mr. Calvin McRae
by Rev. Wm. F. Carmichael

I'm just a man
So I am subject to error
Yet I look forward
To a day much fairer
I give my best
By faith I shall give better
Justice to all
Regardless of the matter
I'm just a man
One day I will be better.

I gave my family life
I gave what God gave me
Sometimes there was some strife
But I am just a man, you see
I loved through deeds
I tried to please
To give you love, comfort, possessions
I know there can be no regressions
I gave you an imperfect stand
I am just a mortal man

Forgive my faults
Love me, in spite of my failure
See my intent
Don't let the facts assail you
For struggling inside
Of me there is a Hebrew
Promising me

That one day I shall be brand new
Forgive my faults
As I forgive yours too.

I'm just a man
I'm limited in time
I'm limited in patience
I'm limited and blind
Some things I see
I cannot see it all
Please pick me up
When I stumble and fall
After all
I'm just a mortal man.

Excellency

1922-2005

9-21-05
To Gladys Carmichael/Monroe

We called you Mother
Because of how you taught us
For your mental strategy
You deserve an A plus

You directed by leading
Never did you force us
You gave us choices
To decide whatever we discussed

They named you Gladys
They called you Gla
Your spirit was cheerful
Every sunny and stormy day
Your hopes were strong
You cleared our way

Gladys Bowen/Carmichael/Monroe
We grade you with the highest score
Yet Jesus Christ will grade you more
You're now upon His beautiful shore
You'll now experience,
Hope fulfilled as you explore
The Joy and Gladness of Heaven CORE

You loved us so
Everyday we'll Love and miss you more.

Our French Teacher – Mom Foxworth
by Rev. Wm. F. Carmichael – 1990
in Memory of Mrs. Willie B. Foxworth
March 4, 1918 – Dec. 15, 1990

Aurevoir Aurevoir

Mon Professeur de Francais

You were more than a teacher
We called you Mom
When others could not reach us
You opened your arms
If just a stare... it was heeded
No physical force at all was needed
You gave us pure love.... without harm
We honored you with the title mom

Where principals failed you succeeded
Your love commanded it never pleaded
Your direction exceeded our time of training
Though years have past it is still remaining
Higher learning we have obtained
You provided for us the frame
We hail you...... you earned your name
Farewell Mom Foxworth we all exclaim
Farewell........ Mom Professeur Foxworth

Sister Martha Smallwood

"My stepmother did not treat me good"
Was the words of Martha Smallwood,
A personal, precious loving one,
Decided when adult life had begun.
To make a home and a loving home she made,
"That of her daughter; it would never be said,"
My mother did not treat me good.

She gave the love she did not receive.
For in her heart she did believe
That every child which walked and breathe,
Should know love and loving deeds
The giving of candy was her expression
When her mind did foster regression
To children close and even some distant
For in loving children she had no resistance.

She gave her life to God above
He gave her His eternal love
Called her home to rest in peace
Thoughts of regression at last to cease
Though loving deeds they still do linger
In hearts of children as they remember
A little woman named, Martha Smallwood
Always, always doing them good.
May God bless Sister Smallwood.

A Concerned Daughter

2-26-2010

A grown daughter and mother has a phone conversation with her Mother about her beloved Daddy she sees her dreams fading away.

In memory of Uncle John Arch's
Home Mad Train
John Arch Anderson

Ma! ..... Ma!! ..... Ma!!!
Did you know Daddy's got a little baby...?
Not in that big stomach of his ... Ma
Don't worry he doesn't have another lady
But ... Daddy's got a little baby
No Ma, ... You know he's been faithful to you
Hard as he works he ain't got time for foolishness

Ma!...
Daddy has carried an idea for years
He's in labor
You see those quiet tears he sheds
He's been carrying that thing for years
He can't deliver it by hisself
He needs you Ma,
To tell him how to breathe
I don't know when that thing was conceived
He needs you, Ma

Ma, build up his faith to
believe in hisself
Don't tear him down
He's about to deliver
Don't let nobody steal it
Don't let it die before it's born

Sarah Margaret

1832-1940

A slave's story McNeil Bullard Anderson   3-10-2010

When I was only twelve years old
I was stolen, I was sold
I was taken from my homeland
To the land of the white man

I was forced to board a ship
My spirit within was torn and ripped
Surely my heart did skip a beat
When in my struggle I suffered defeat

My dreams all died, my future uncertain
I was surrounded by a dark, dark curtain
Charleston South Carolina I, see
In the bidding house, they sold me

I grew up very fast
I had to survive I had to last
I had to overcome my fears
I had to function beyond my years

I married a man, had a family
Worked in the fields where ever I'd be
Washed our clothes cooked our meals
Nursed my children when they were ill

Sold twice in a slavery state
Now I be 108

1940 is the year
Many have died yet I'm still here

I'm ready for Jesus to take me home
To the family where I belong
I have kept the faith, I have been strong
In body and spirit I have grown

Old ship of Zion I welcome you
This life of slavery is through
I get aboard of my own will
Sail me high above the hills
To my Jesus I belong
To my Jesus freedom's home

Reflections To Aunt Francis McLean

I just wanted to take a second
To stop along the way
To pick just a few of the flowers of life
You planted yesterday
Now they make up your bouquet

The times in life you thought of me
When I was not thinking of you
The numbers of times you prepared my meals
This is the least that I can do
Aunt Francis I love you

You've washed my clothes
You've been my mom
You've given shelter for my head
In many little simple ways
You've made my heart so glad.

You made a lovely beautiful home
You than invited me in
This you did not have to do
But you did and you'd do it again
From the love you store within.

Daring not to forget your spouse
For he provided you the house
Put food on the family's table
Your love helped to make him able
Your love did keep him stable

For your loving ways
I give you praise
For patience, hope, and care
If ever I needed a tender heart
Aunt Francis you were there.
These precious reflections,
Aunt Francis you share.

Memories Of Bro. Stewart

1898-1968

The Unison Of Life And Death

There's a unison twixt life and death,
    That man doesn't understand,
There's a knowledge of the ever-existence God
    That, seems to give command.

There's a pathway leading to Holy Chambers
    Which only the righteous can trod
Our spiritual brother, has been chosen.
    To now, dwell in the house God.

Through death, there's unison great than it was before,
    For now he's entered the spiritual door.
Having been faithful to the path he trod,
    He's been released from this land

Through natural sorrow, try and see.
    He's now with God forever to be
Where grief nor misery cannot enter in
    Without a spot of tormenting sin

Prepare, prepare, God would speak to you.
    For our dear brother Stewart has made it through.
Rejoice fo him, on this reminscent day.
    Thank God Almighty, He found the way

Prepare, prepare, to join him one day
    Havin, fulfiled your ministry,
To join our Father in unity.

James (Jim) Bowens

1898-1984

A Teacher

God gave us wisdom through James Bowen
He fought to teach the way
Inspired by the Holy Spirit
He taught in forceful display
With all the strength God gave him
Words and action did convey
Obey God rather than man
Not just on Sunday, but every day.

He was a teacher, he was a leader
This man could clearly see
In his life was the word Himself in
Pure reality
Yes, he was subject to error
As everyone from earth
He had an active temper
Sometimes with loud outbursts

He said he was "Jim Minded"
Others could not see as he
God blessed him in the life he lived
A life of Christianity
Educated enough to teach public school

But never followed it through
Counted teaching in church a greater glory
Than would have I or you

God has made him finite
A more powerful force he'll be
One day he'll command angels
In the forever eternity
One day he will be crowned
For the energy he used on earth
Energy used in many ways
To promote God's kingdom first
James Jim Bowen
Through death unto new birth.

Deacon Henry Brown

1911-1999

A Faithful Man

A watchful man to guide us
A long a risky way
A trustful man to take care us
Through every earthly day
A powerful man to command us
That we not go astray
Was faithful in his duties
Retired from us today
We need not mourn his leaving
He served his capacity
He gave us what he had been given
He showed us how faith should be
Persistent in its achieving
To fashion reality
To stand, and stand, and stand
Amid adversity

Almighty God saw he was faithful
In spite of him being human
God prepared away for him
To search out a distant land

Harvey McCallum

Pray For Me

"Rev Carmichael pray for me"?
"Rev Carmichael pray for me"?
Those were the words of Harvey

He wanted God to know it all
Most of all, to know the cause
He wanted someone to plead his case
So his life would not be a waste
Rev. Carmichael, pray in my place

I am burdened now, pray for me
I am a slave to booz, pray for me
I am treated wrong, pray for me
I am misunderstood, pray for me
That I might do good
Rev. Carmichael, pray for me!
That I be set free
"Rev Carmichael, it's your job
Pray for me"!

Knowing he was dependable
He would follow to the end
And leave a marker along the way
Where we too, could begin

A Crown of Glory

To Pastor John L. Meares for 50 years plus service
By a son of your ministry.......Pastor Wm. F. Carmichael
1PE. 5:4

From Tennessee to Washington D.C.
God sent a young man one day
Not to be President
To show God's people the way

A Light to be in the Capital
Men would sing Hellaluiah
A father to Pastors from afar
A Bishop of Bishops is who you are

From Florida to Maine
Men would hear and see your fame
Greater than a President
A called and chosen son, God sent

To rule in the Kingdom at Washington D.C.
To defeat the powers of promiscuity
A man of faith, a man of prayer
A son of God a victorious preacher
Storing up treasures in heavenly places
Overcoming in all your races
Silver, gold and precious stones
To you one day around Christ's throne

A Sermon

A testimony in memory of Mr. Sam Alford, a new convert

"Call Him up, tell Him what you want!!"
A son used to say.
As son of God gone on to glory
He's with the Lord today.

He was born of God in the usual way
He was born of God late in the day
He had a debt he had to pay
He had to suffer in this body of clay
He was born of God in great array.

"Call Him up, tell Him what you want."
The only sermon he preached.
He preached it to be Ones he loved
So they would know who to seek.
He worked hard, to take care of you
His family on this Earth
Knowing that God would call him Home
He tried to prepare *you* first.

Knowing that many of you need to change
Your goals you need to rearrange.
Or you won't see him on that day
When crowned with a body, not made of clay.
You need to get to know the Man
The Man Jesus who's got a plan
To take you on from earth to glory
Where Sam Alford shall end his story.

Call Him up!!
And if He knows you,
Don't worry, your message it will get through
If He knows you, He knows what you want
Your life on earth He will anoint
To give you peace with every man
To banish the evil which you have planned
To turn you from your selfish way
Unto the way of a perfect day
Call Him up!!
Then, bow down and pray.

You can see Sam Alford again
If you know God in the pardon of your sins
You can see Sam after Judgement Day
If what you want is the righteous way
"Call Him up tell Him what you want"
He will not with good things taunt.
"Call Him up, tell Him what you want."

Just A Mortal Man

In Memories of Mr. Calvin McRae
by Rev. Wm. F. Carmichael

I'm just a man
So I am subject to error
Yet I look forward
To a day much fairer
I give my best
by faith I shall give better
Justice to all
Regardless of the matter
I'm just a man
One day I will be better.

I gave my family life
I gave what God gave me
Sometimes there was some strife
But I am just a man, you see
I loved through deeds
I tried to please
To give you love, comfort, possessions
I know there can be no regressions
I gave you an imperfect stand
I am just a mortal man

Forgive my faults
Love me, in spite of my failure
See my intent
Don't let the facts assail you
For struggling inside
Of me there is a Hebrew
Promising me

That one day I shall be brand new
Forgive my faults
As I forgive yours too.

I'm just a man
I'm limited in time
I'm limited in patience
I'm limited and blind
Some things I see
I cannot see it all
Please pick me up
When I stumble and fall
After all
I'm just a mortal man.

Miss Polly

A Lumbee 1988

Fish need water to swim
Birds need air to fly
So was needed Miss Polly
Her children was her life

She gave her love so freely
Asked nothing in return
In everything she said and did
She showed she was concerned

She gave us what she knew
To guide us this lif through
She will live in her children
By the things she taught us to do

If you knew her you knew her mind
For she spoke it boldly and clear
And if needs be, she spoke it loudly
To those who were hard to hear
She lived she loved she suffered she died
She was so happy, she burst in tears and cried
Now God shall wipe away her tears
And rest her weary eyes
And give Miss Polly happiness
That will last forever inside

The Journey's End

For Bessie Percell

I met a lady that knew Jesus
Just a year ago
She was kind and good to all
Just like Jesus told her to be so

She was always with a smile
Giving a kind word or two
There was nothing which she had
That was too good to give to you

She was here and my best friend here
She proved her love to God and me each day
In prayer
That's why I know Jesus
Has taken her aboard with care

Sleep on my friend and take your rest
We'll miss you here, we know you've done your best
Now rest.

To My Darling Grandmother

Adoration
Magnolia Anderson-Bowens 1900-1994

I love you, I love you
My darling Grandmother.
I love you, I love you,
My darling Grandmother.
For your prayers I'm sure did save me

I honor you, I honor you,
Yes, honor is due.
And just as a person.
I adore you too.
I love you, I love you,
My darling Grandmother
I love you, yes I do.

I exalt you, I exalt you.
You're worthy to be lifted up.
You've stood the storms,
Like a tree by the river.
Salvation to me, you helped deliver
I exalt you, I exalt you
My darling Grandmother
You are worthy indeed to be praised.

Awakened to life,
You helped awake me.
Awakened to Christ,
You helped me to see.

Awakened to spirit,
You fed my soul,
Awakened to God,
You sought my goal.
I love you, love you
My darling Grandmother.
With a godly love that shall
Never grow cold.

Mother

You taught us to say Mother
Our hearts desired none other
When children were saying mom & mama
You taught us to say mother

You give us dignity
Imparted in us a quality
A special difference you cannot see
You gave us dignity

In ways which seemed so simple
The hardships of life could never crimple
As though without a blemish or pimple
You made life seem so simple

You labored in love and love succeeded
You chastened you counseled,
You even pleaded
You mounted up to what was needed
You labored in love and love succeeded.
Not only to us, but also others
You walked worthy of your title Mother

Dorothy (Ford) Lee

1945 –

My Desire

Lord let me teach
Someone the way
How to work and how to play
How to achieve day by day
Lord, let me teach

Lord, let me help
Someone to read
To spell, each word with rapid speed
To equip the youth with what they need
Lord, let me help

Lord, I don't know
Teach me
Lord, I can't see
Lead me
Lord, I'm not what I need to be
I try my best, to depend on thee
Lord, I don't know
Teach me

When all teaching is done
I'll shine bright as the sun
If I've turned someone from wrong to right
I'll be rewarded in thy sight
Like the stars in heaven's above
If I turn them to your love
Then I have taught

Burden Carrier

Some carry their burdens on their heads
You see their sorrow first of all

Some carry their burdens on their shoulders
Then they don't seem so tall

Some carry their burdens on their backs
The very last thing you see

They want of you first to get to
Know them not their suffering

Helen Smith carried burdens
Although she did not broadcast it
Each day they were heavier and heavier
Yet Helen didn't quit
She carried her burdens in the heat of the day
Until the Lord called her away
No grumbling or complaining did she do
Now her laboring is through
She's now laughing instead of crying
She's now living instead of dying
She's now singing instead of mourning
Heaven to her is now dawning
On the other shore

Until

11-12-20-10

I won't see you again until another
So let's remember happy days gone by
When you laughed so hard it made you cry
When we hugged so tight the breath almost left us
Even those joyous endings that started with a fuss

The way you walked and especially how you ran
The way you talked and how your sentences began
The colors you loved to were the type of flowers you loved
The jokes you told or tried to tell that made you shrug

The foods you could never get enough of
During holiday seasons, how you held that egg nog jug
The way your mouth would sometimes look so funny
How you rolled your eyes when you thought someone was a dummy
How fast you would come to other's defense or not
How you expressed joy when you found what was sought

Let us be friends, let us be friends,
Let us be friends
Until we meet, again
When cherry blossoms bloom,
When tulips sprout and lilacs perfume the air
Let us comtemplate and converase on things that really care

About the Author

William Carmichael a lifelong - learner always wanted to share what he had learned. For many years, he would put on a Black History Exhibit on Rowland's Main Street in Rowland, NC. When he stopped sharing the exhibit on Main Street, he took it to local schools and had engaging assemblies with the students.

His most important job was as a servant for the Lord. One of his most talked about jobs was one that he had at the White House during President Jimmy Carter's administration.

He was the founder of family of God Ministries, Inc. In later years, he devoted most of his servitude to Abundant Life Ministries, and Mt Tabor Baptist Church.

Throughout his life poetry is being written

Barbara A. Carmichael
Family of God Ministries